DISASTERS

CHALLENGER and COLUMBIA

Kathleen Fahey

GARETH**STEVENS**
GS
PUBLISHING
A WRC Media Company

Please visit our web site at: **www.garethstevens.com**
For a free color catalog describing Gareth Stevens Publishing's list
of high-quality books and multimedia programs, call 1-800-542-2595 (USA)
or 1-800-387-3178 (Canada). Gareth Stevens Publishing's fax: (414) 332-3567.

Library of Congress Cataloging-in-Publication Data

Fahey, Kathleen, 1961-
      Challenger and Columbia / Kathleen Fahey.
          p. cm. — (Disasters)
      Includes bibliographical references and index.
      ISBN 0-8368-4496-3 (lib. bdg.)
      1. Challenger (Spacecraft)—Accidents—Juvenile literature. 2. Columbia
(Spacecraft)—Accidents—Juvenile literature. 3. Space shuttles—Accidents—
United States—Juvenile literature. I. Title. II. Disasters (Milwaukee, Wis.)
      TL867.F34   2005
      363.12'465'0973—dc22   2004056706

This edition first published in 2005 by
Gareth Stevens Publishing
A WRC Media Company
330 West Olive Street, Suite 100
Milwaukee, Wisconsin 53212 USA

Original copyright © 2004 The Brown Reference Group plc. This U.S. edition
copyright © 2005 by Gareth Stevens, Inc.

Project Editor: Tim Cooke
Consultant: Don Franceschetti, Distinguished Service Professor, Departments
of Physics and Chemistry, University of Memphis, Tennessee
Designer: Lynne Ross
Picture Researcher: Becky Cox

Gareth Stevens series editor: Jenette Donovan Guntly
Gareth Stevens art direction: Tammy West

Picture credits: Front Cover: Corbis
Corbis title page, Bettmann 9, 16, NASA 10, Roger Ressmeyer 22, Reuters/ POOL/
Eric Gay 24, Ross Pictures 23; NASA: 11, 12, 13, DFRC 27, Human Space Flight 19,
Johnson Space Center 6, 7, 15, 17, 25, 26, Kennedy Space Center 5, 8, 14, 20, 28,
USGS 29; Rex Features: 18; Science Photo Library: James L. Amos/ Peter Arnold 21.

Maps and Artwork: Brown Reference Group plc

Printed in the United States of America

1 2 3 4 5 6 7 8 9 09 08 07 06 05

ABOUT THE AUTHOR

American-born Kathleen Fahey has been writing children's books on a
wide range of subjects for over fifteen years. She now lives in England
with her young family, who "test-drive" all of her books.

CONTENTS

1 DISASTERS IN SPACE

The National Aeronautical and Space Agency (NASA) runs space exploration in the United States. In 1969, NASA put the first person on the moon. It also began to build space shuttles to fly into space regularly. Then, in 1986, the shuttle program was hit by a disaster.

The seven **astronauts** of the space shuttle *Challenger* waited for days at Cape Canaveral before liftoff. The mission was put off several times for reasons ranging from problems with machinery to bad weather. At last, at 11:38 A.M. EST (Eastern Standard Time) on January 28, 1986, *Challenger*'s **booster** rockets fired. With a huge thrust, *Challenger* left the launch pad and rose into the sky.

Crowds of people watched in the winter morning air at the Kennedy Space Center in Cape Canaveral, Florida. Television viewers tuned in around the world to watch the launch, including hundreds of thousands of U.S. schoolchildren. Only 73 seconds into the mission, *Challenger* exploded. The entire crew died. At the time, it was the worst disaster in the history of the space program. People everywhere were shocked by the tragedy.

▶ The space shuttle *Challenger* takes off from Cape Canaveral in Florida on its last flight. The shuttle was powered by the brown-colored tank, which held liquid nitrogen and oxygen fuel that catches fire very easily. It also had two white booster rockets, one of which can be seen here.

4

▲ **Teacher Christa McAuliffe floats in the air during her training. NASA uses special aircraft to create the conditions astronauts face in space, where there is very little gravity.**

The shuttle program's aim was to develop spacecraft that could carry equipment into space. *Columbia*, the first space shuttle, was launched in 1981. By 1986, there had been nine more successful shuttle **missions**.

TRAGEDY IN SPACE

People were more interested in *Challenger* than in any event since the launch of *Columbia*. Many people followed the preparations for the flight. *Challenger* was carrying Christa McAuliffe, the first member of the Teacher in Space Program. She was a high-school teacher from Concord, New Hampshire. McAuliffe would be the first American civilian to fly in space.

Christa was picked from eleven thousand people for the *Challenger* mission. She trained for a year as an astronaut with NASA. Students throughout the country followed McAuliffe's progress on TV as she got ready for the flight.

Challenger's mission was to put **satellites** into place. The satellites would help astronomers, who are scientists who study

THE ASTRONAUTS ABOARD CHALLENGER

Leading the *Challenger* crew was the commander, Francis "Dick" Scobee, who had already flown on a shuttle mission. Michael J. Smith was the pilot; *Challenger* was his first space flight. With them were Ronald E. McNair, Judith A. Resnik, and Ellison S. Onizuka. They were scientists who would make sure the shuttle worked properly and also carry out experiments in space. The **payload** specialists, who looked after the equipment the shuttle would put into space, were Gregory B. Jarvis and teacher Christa McAuliffe. All seven people had lots of training for the mission. After the disaster, their families formed the Challenger Organization in their memory. It gives money to Challenger Learning Centers to encourage students to find out about space. The Ronald McNair Foundation also encourages scientific study.

▼ The *Challenger* crew: back row (from left to right): Ellison S. Onizuka, Christa McAuliffe, Gregory B. Jarvis, Judith A. Resnik; front row (from left to right): Michael J. Smith, Francis "Dick" Scobee, and Ronald E. McNair.

► Burning pieces from *Challenger* created smoke trails in the sky moments after the spacecraft exploded.

EYEWITNESS

"Christa was a mentor to me and a hero to my students. That day I stood on the lawn outside looking expectantly into the sky with 33 students around me. We all waited excitedly and the children squealed with delight when the Challenger *came into view on the horizon. Then we noticed the white smoke and the split Y pattern in the sky. I knew in my heart something was terribly wrong. The children all started to ask what was happening, but I was afraid to answer."*

— KATHLEEN ALLEY

space, follow Halley's comet. A comet is a large lump of ice and rock that circles around the Sun. Halley's comet passes near Earth every seventy-six years.

Everything should have gone well, but as the liftoff date neared, many things began to go wrong. The launch was planned for 3:43 P.M. on January 22, 1986. It was moved to January 23, January 24, and then to January 25 due to bad weather. Then, problems with machinery and more bad weather delayed the launch until January 28. After the disaster, many people asked if the doomed mission should have gone ahead at all.

► **People watching the takeoff were horrified when the shuttle blew up. Among the watchers were some family members of the astronauts on board *Challenger*.**

FACT FILE

CHALLENGER

WHERE: Above Cape Canaveral, Florida

WHEN: January 28, 1986

DAMAGE: Completely blown apart

COSTS: About $500 million

KILLED: Seven dead

COLUMBIA

WHERE: Above Texas and Louisiana

WHEN: February 1, 2003

DAMAGE: Completely blown apart

COSTS: About $500 million

KILLED: Seven dead

The *Challenger* tragedy led to the shuttle program being stopped for almost three years. NASA created better safety systems to stop future disasters. Space shuttle flights began again in September 1988. Fifteen years later, another tragedy hit. The shuttle *Columbia* fell apart as it reentered the Earth's **atmosphere**.

A SECOND DISASTER

The seven *Columbia* astronauts were almost home when disaster struck. They had spent sixteen days in space, doing more than eighty

▲ **This image shows a space shuttle floating in space above Earth in 1995. The doors of the shuttle's cargo bay are open, because a satellite has just been put into orbit.**

scientific tests. They were due to land at 9:16 A.M. EST on February 1, 2003. Just before 9:00 A.M., the crew was getting ready for the final part of the spacecraft's journey over Texas before landing in Florida.

The flight was being guided by NASA Mission Control in Houston, Texas. Mission Control noticed a problem with data about the temperature on the shuttle's left wing. There were also problems with the meters that read the pressure of the tires on the left side of the

THE COLUMBIA CREW

▼ The *Columbia* crew: top row (from left to right): David Brown, William McCool, Michael Anderson; bottom row (from left to right): Kalpana Chawla, Rick Husband, Laurel Clark, and Ilan Ramon.

The *Columbia* mission was led by commander Rick Husband, an astronaut who had already flown on one space mission. He was joined by pilot William "Willie" McCool and mission specialists Kalpana Chawla, Laurel Clark, Michael Anderson, and David Brown. They would do a number of scientific tests. Also on board was payload specialist Ilan Ramon, who was the first person from Israel to go into space. Dr. Kalpana Chawla was another first: the first woman from India in space. People from all around the world, especially in India and Israel, mourned the loss of *Columbia* along with the United States.

shuttle's wheels for landing. No one was too worried. They thought there might be a small problem with the **communications system**. Mission Control sent a radio message to the shuttle: "*Columbia*, [this is] Houston. We see your tire pressure messages and we did not copy [understand] your last [message]."

Mission commander Rick Husband replied "Roger, uh, b[ut] . . . ." Then there was silence, and some static, or hissing noises. Mission Control thought this was due to the shuttle reentering the atmosphere, which breaks up radio signals. When they could not get back in touch with the shuttle, however, they knew that something was seriously wrong.

Moments later, the space shuttle broke into pieces as it reentered the Earth's atmosphere at a speed of 12,500 miles (20,100 kilometers)

▲ **Michael Anderson reads a checklist during the *Columbia* flight. Anderson's job was to look after a lot of the equipment on board the spacecraft.**

per hour. It blew apart over Texas and Louisiana. Parts of the shuttle rained down on parts of those states and Arkansas. It missed any large towns or cities, but thousands of people found **debris** in their back yards. Emergency telephone lines were kept busy as people called in to report seeing the accident.

NASA, the Federal Bureau of Investigation (FBI), and soldiers from the National Guard sent out teams to collect the debris. They thought the pieces might provide clues about the cause of the disaster. They told the public not to touch the debris in case it had harmful chemicals on it from the shuttle. Meanwhile, the shuttle program was stopped again, as it had been after the *Challenger* disaster in 1986.

EYEWITNESS

"As we saw Columbia coming over, we saw a lot of light and it looked like debris and stuff was coming off the shuttle. We saw large masses of pieces coming off the shuttle as it was coming by. Then the house kind of shook and we noticed a sonic boom . . . and then we saw a big continuous puff of vapor or smoke stream come out and then we noticed a big chunk go over."

— BENJAMIN LASTER

KEMP, TEXAS

◄ **Well wishers pay their respects to the *Columbia* astronauts on the day of the disaster. Mourners left flowers, cards, and balloons outside the Johnson Space Center in Houston, Texas.**

2 THE CAUSES OF THE DISASTERS

Experts investigated both the space shuttle disasters. Both accidents were caused by failures of equipment. Experts also looked at all of NASA, however. They found faults in how much money NASA was given and how the agency was run.

After the 1986 *Challenger* disaster, President Ronald Reagan set up a **commission** to find the cause of the accident. It was named the Rogers Commission for its head, William Rogers. While the investigation went on, search teams used nets to search the ocean off the Florida coast. They were looking for any debris from the shuttle that might give clues about why it exploded.

▼ **This piece of one of Challenger's solid-fuel booster rockets was found after the accident. The damage to it suggested to scientists that the "O-ring" had failed.**

THE DAMAGED PART

The commission's report was released on June 6, 1986. It blamed the disaster on the failure of an "O-ring," a round **seal**, located in the booster rocket on *Challenger*'s right side. The design

In this photograph, taken just before the shuttle blew up, a flame is visible from *Challenger*'s booster rocket, on the right above the main smoke trail. The flame shows that there was a hole in the rocket.

of the seal, combined with the effects of the very cold weather on launch day, meant that the seal was not airtight. Flames from the booster rocket passed through it. They burned through *Challenger*'s outside fuel tank and the supports that held the tank to the booster rocket. The booster rocket smashed into the fuel tank. Liquid hydrogen and oxygen fuel from the tank and the booster mixed together and caught fire. The explosion that followed blew the shuttle to pieces.

In addition to the physical causes of the disaster, the commission looked at other

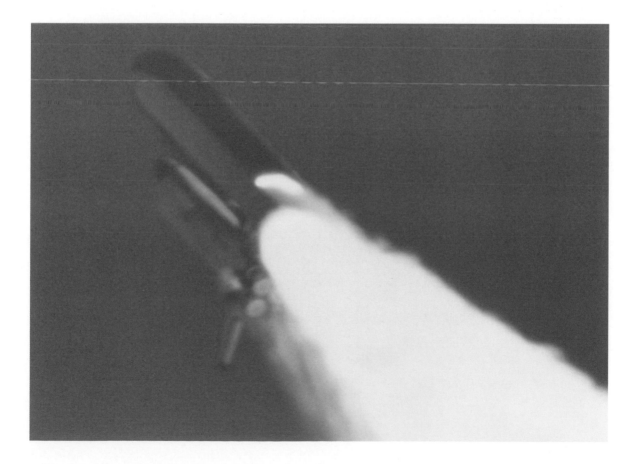

THE ROGERS COMMISSION

There were fourteen members of the commission set up by President Ronald Reagan to look at the causes of the *Challenger* disaster. The head of the commission, William Rogers, had served in the government as a former **secretary of state**. With him on the commission were many experts who knew the space program well. They included Neil Armstrong, who was the first man to walk on the moon, and Sally Ride, who was the first female astronaut. The commission also included Chuck Yeager, who was a famous pilot who had tested aircraft for the U.S. Air Force. Yeager had made many test flights to help start the space program, before NASA had trained any astronauts.

The commission held thirty-five meetings to talk to NASA experts and read about twenty thousand pages of documents before writing its report. It took them six months.

▼ **Members of the Rogers Commission hold a meeting for reporters. In the front row, from left to right, are former astronaut Neil Armstrong; William Rogers, who was the head of the commission; and astronaut Sally Ride.**

NEIL ARMSTRONG   WILLIAM ROGERS   SALLY RIDE

▼ **Workers lower a piece from the *Challenger* into an old missile silo, a deep hole for storing missiles, at Cape Canaveral, Florida. Most of the parts of the shuttle were buried.**

problems with the mission. The team wanted to find out why the "O-ring" problem had been missed and why NASA managers let the mission go ahead. Some NASA experts had been worried about the shuttle's safety, but the launch had been allowed anyway. The commission found fault with the officials at NASA who let the launch go ahead.

The shuttle program was stopped. It could not start again until there were changes to the shuttle. NASA managers also had to improve the way they checked to be sure that all parts of the shuttle were safe. Shuttle missions began again on September 28, 1988, with the flight of the shuttle *Discovery*.

CAUSES OF THE SECOND DISASTER

Despite the new safety measures, tragedy struck again with the loss of the shuttle *Columbia* in February 2003.

FOX NEWS ALERT

▲ **This picture from Fox News shows debris from** *Columbia* **burning on the ground.**

Again, after the accident, fault was found with how NASA was run. Some space experts asked whether the U.S. government wanted to explore space badly enough to spend the money it took to ensure safety.

On February 1, 2003, only four hours after *Columbia* was lost, NASA official Sean O'Keefe created the Columbia Accident Investigation Board (CAIB). The CAIB's job was to study the causes of the disaster and report on what could be done to ensure the safety of future shuttle missions. The board published its report seven months later.

The CAIB found that the direct cause of the *Columbia* breakup was the failure of a seal on the shuttle's left wing. The seal had been damaged during liftoff. It was struck by a piece of foam **insulation** that came loose from the shuttle's outside fuel tank. The seal fell off the shuttle the next day. This left a gap that let hot gas into the shuttle during its reentry into the Earth's atmosphere, which made the shuttle blow apart. The CAIB studied an identical fuel tank on another shuttle. It found many faults in

▶ **NASA official Sean O'Keefe talks to NASA employees the week after the *Columbia* disaster. O'Keefe set up the Columbia Accident Investigation Board (CAIB) to discover the causes of the accident.**

▲ **This photograph from March 2003 shows pieces from *Columbia* laid out to show where they came from on the shuttle. Experts put together what they could of *Columbia* to try to find out what had happened to it.**

the tank's outer cover. One board member said, "In four simple words, the foam did it."

The CAIB also studied the background of the disaster. It decided that the attitude of the government and NASA officials meant that the space program did not have enough money. The government had tried to get NASA to save money and stick to the schedule for the shuttle program. NASA managers were more interested in keeping costs down and meeting set dates than they were with ensuring the safety of the shuttles.

The board said some problems in both the *Columbia* and *Challenger* disasters were the same. In both cases, it said, NASA managers should or could have realized that the risks

THE PROBLEM WITH THE FOAM

NASA staff were aware that some foam had broken away from *Columbia*'s outside booster rocket on liftoff and had hit the shuttle's left wing. They played the accident down, however, and did not look into it further. They believed that the accident had not done much damage to the shuttle and was not very important. They also knew that, even if the wing had been damaged, there was nothing anyone could do to repair it. Looking back, it is clear that the damage was very serious. The CAIB insisted that NASA come up with new ways for shuttle crews to study and repair any damage to their shuttles while in flight. These methods have to be in place before any shuttles are allowed to fly again.

▼ A NASA worker checks insulation tiles on the *Columbia* before its mission. A loose tile damaged the shuttle wing on takeoff.

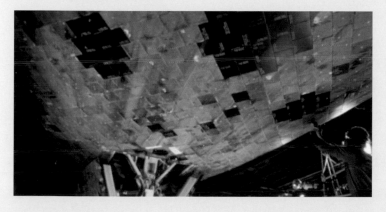

were too great. They could have performed better checks, gotten more data, and listened to people's concerns. They also could have asked more questions about information they were given.

The CAIB also found that the lessons NASA had learned from the *Challenger* disaster had been ignored or forgotten. All shuttle flights were again stopped while NASA made the changes outlined in the CAIB report.

3 AFTERMATH OF THE DISASTERS

A number of changes took place after the *Challenger* disaster, but they did not stop the *Columbia* disaster from happening. After the second accident, NASA tried even harder to make space shuttles safer.

Following the *Challenger* disaster in 1986, shuttle flights were stopped. NASA made the changes asked for by the Rogers Commission, including changing the design of the shuttles. The changes also included a redesign of the "O-rings," which were the main direct cause of the disaster. NASA managers

▼ **The doomed *Columbia* is improved after the *Challenger* disaster. All of NASA's shuttles were completely looked over and repaired after the accident.**

had to put into place better quality controls as well. The new way of working would help to ensure that no shuttle parts had any weaknesses. Also, more people who had been astronauts themselves and who had traveled into space were given management positions at NASA.

NASA was also told to stop using parts taken from one shuttle to repair another. It had to keep a supply of spares, no matter what the cost. The changes were intended to make the program safer and to avoid future disasters.

IS SPACE WORTH IT?

The *Challenger* disaster had a huge impact. People throughout the United States and around the world saw the tragedy on live television. They saw the horror of the astronauts' families, who were at the launch. Students who were fans of Christa McAuliffe never forgot the shock of her death. For many children, it was the first time they had lost someone who was like a friend. One student said, "The world stopped when the *Challenger* exploded." Students today are reminded of the tragedy by visiting Challenger Learning Centers, which allow students to see what it is like to be part of a shuttle crew.

▲ **This memorial to the *Challenger* crew stands at Arlington National Cemetery in Virginia. The disaster made a great impact on many Americans, who saw it happen live on television.**

The disaster reminded people that space travel is still risky. Americans had been proud when the Apollo space program put a human on the Moon in the 1960s. The *Challenger* disaster made many people wonder whether exploring space is really so important.

AFTERMATH OF THE SECOND DISASTER

The Columbia Accident Investigation Board (CAIB) found that some of the lessons of the *Challenger* disaster had been forgotten. There had been cuts in NASA's budget. The agency had dates for its work that were hard to meet, which made it difficult for the shuttle program to meet high safety standards.

The report listed many things that NASA had to do before it would be allowed to start

▲ A chunk of foam breaks up after being fired at a piece of a shuttle wing. This test was done after the *Columbia* disaster. It showed that a loose piece of foam could have cracked *Columbia*'s wing.

shuttle flights again. One important change is to make it possible for astronauts to repair damage to the outside of the shuttle while it is in space. The shuttles must also have cameras that can see any damage to the tiles on the

THE INTERNATIONAL SPACE STATION

An important future use for the space shuttle will be to carry crews to and from the International Space Station (ISS). The ISS is being built by the United States and sixteen other nations. It is in orbit about 250 miles (400 kilometers) above Earth. The first sections were launched in 1998 and the first crew arrived in 2000. Scientists will be able to live in the ISS for months at a time, doing tests about how being in space changes the human body.

▼ **This painting shows what the finished International Space Station (ISS) will look like when all its sections are put together in about 2010.**

▼ An astronaut uses a robot arm to move around outside the shuttle. In the future, equipment such as this will allow astronauts to repair any damage to the shuttle while it is in space.

outside of the shuttle. The foam insulation that caused the damage to *Columbia*'s wing will be redesigned so that it is stronger and does not break off during liftoff. The way that NASA managers work together will improve because they must be more careful to share information quickly with everyone who needs it. The landing path of the space shuttle also has to be changed so that it does not go over areas where many people live. The path of *Columbia* took it over large towns. It was only by good

THE CREW EXPLORATION VEHICLE

The original space shuttle was designed in the 1970s. Science has advanced a lot since then. The shuttles have been improved since the first flight in 1981, but some aerospace experts, who are people who design aircraft and spacecraft, believe that it is time for a completely new design. Current plans are to stop using the space shuttle by 2010, when the International Space Station (ISS) is fully finished. The shuttle will be replaced by a new spaceship, known as the Crew Exploration Vehicle (CEV). The CEV is due to be tested in 2008, but many experts who are watching the program think that the CEV will not be ready by then.

The CEV will be able to fly back and forth between the ISS and Earth and also to the Moon. In order to power the CEV, however, NASA will have to develop "heavy lifter" rockets. These powerful rockets would be capable of lifting much heavier loads than current rockets can. The CEV would also have to carry a huge amount of fuel in order to return to Earth from the ISS. Whether NASA will be able to overcome these problems still remains to be seen. In 2004, President George W. Bush called for more money to be available for NASA.

▼ A smaller model of the Crew Exploration Vehicle (CEV) is unloaded from a transport plane for tests in 2000.

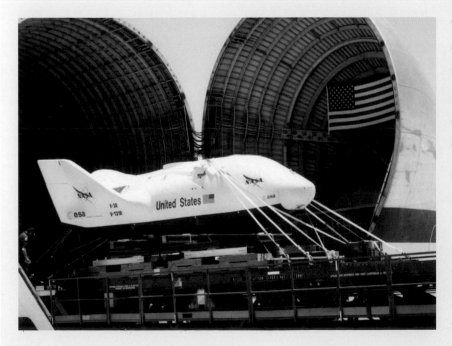

27

luck that parts from the shuttle did not kill or injure people on the ground.

In 2004, NASA had decided that the shuttle program would not begin again before March 2005. The shuttle *Discovery* is due to travel to the International Space Station to test the new repair methods. Barbara Morgan, a teacher who now works for NASA full time, will be on board as part of the Teacher in Space Program.

In 2004, President George W. Bush called for the government to increase how much money NASA receives by $1 billion over five years. The money would pay for missions to the Moon and to Mars. It would also help make sure the shuttle was safe enough to play a role in the next great steps in space exploration.

▼ The space shuttle *Atlantis* lands at NASA's Kennedy Space Center in Florida in October 2002. After the CAIB report, NASA had to make many changes to how the agency is run before the shuttle program could start again.

WHERE DO WE GO FROM HERE?

People have always wanted to explore the unknown. Traveling in space is one of the greatest challenges still left for human beings. Even though the *Challenger* and *Columbia* disasters made people think twice about space travel, the United States is going to continue its space program.

In 2004, President George W. Bush said that the United States should make more space missions: one to the Moon and another to Mars. No one has ever traveled to Mars. Whether Congress and the American people are willing to pay for such an expensive mission remains to be seen. For now, NASA is mainly working on getting space shuttles back into orbit around Earth.

▼ **Mars, which is also known as the Red Planet for its color, is the nearest planet to Earth. Scientists are working to find a way in which people will one day be able to travel to Mars.**

GLOSSARY

astronauts People who are trained to travel into space.

atmosphere A thick layer of air that surrounds Earth.

booster The part of a rocket that creates the extra power that is needed for liftoff and for the first part of the flight.

commission A group of experts who are brought together in order to do an official duty, such as studying the causes of a disaster.

communications system A system of equipment that allows people aboard spacecraft to get and send messages to and from the Earth.

debris The pieces left when something has been broken up or destroyed.

gravity The natural force that pulls objects toward Earth and makes them feel heavy. There is less gravity in space, so people feel as if they weigh much less.

insulation A layer of material that stops heat from passing through it. Insulation keeps cool objects cool or warm objects warm.

missions Trips that are made to do particular tasks.

payload Objects that are carried by a spacecraft and which are released into space.

orbit A circular path a planet or satellite makes around an object, such as Earth orbiting the Sun.

satellites Machines put into space to circle Earth. Satellites can carry radio and television signals or can take photographs and measure the weather on Earth.

seal A machine part, often made of a rubberlike substance, that stops air or other materials from mixing together where parts join.

secretary of state The U.S. government official in charge of relations with other countries.

FURTHER RESEARCH

BOOKS

Cole, Michael D. *Challenger: America's Space Tragedy (Countdown to Space)*. Enslow Publishers, 1995.

Cole, Michael D. *The Columbia Space Shuttle Disaster: From First Liftoff to Tragic Final Flight*. Enslow Publishers, 2003.

Hansen, Ole Steen. *Space Flight (The Story of Flight)*. Crabtree Publishing Company, 2004.

Hawcock, David. *The Amazing Pop-Up Pull-Out Space Shuttle*. DK Publishing Inc., 1998.

Herrod, Robin. *Space Shuttles (The History of Space Exploration)*. World Almanac Library: 2004.

McNeese, Tim. *The Challenger Disaster*. (Cornerstones of Freedom, second series). Children's Press, 2003.

WEB SITES

Challenger Learning Center Online
www.challenger.org

Howstuffworks, Space Shuttle
science.howstuffworks.com/
space-shuttle.htm

KidsAstronomy.com
www.kidsastronomy.com/
index.htm

NASA Human Spaceflight Space Shuttle
spaceflight.nasa.gov/shuttle/

NASA—Kids' Page
www.nasa.gov/audience/forkids/
home/index.html

World Almanac for Kids— Space Shuttle
www.worldalmanacforkids.com/
explore/space/spaceshuttle.html

INDEX